Soul of Barcelona

30 EXPERIENCES

WRITTEN BY FANY PÉCHIODAT AND VINCENT MOUSTACHE
ILLUSTRATED BY VINCENT MOUSTACHE
PHOTOS BY JUAN JEREZ

JONGLEZ PUBLISHING

Travel guides

‘A THOUSAND PERFUMES
AND A THOUSAND
COLOURS – BARCELONA
IS A CITY OF
A THOUSAND FACES’

JOAN MANUEL SERRAT
“BARCELONA I JO”

WHAT YOU WON'T FIND
IN THIS GUIDE

- a map of the Barcelona Metro
- the direct number for Casa Milà
- the most touristy place for tapas
- a list of medications to bring

WHAT YOU WILL FIND
IN THIS GUIDE

- a breakfast of hot chocolate and charcuterie (where Albert Adrià goes in the morning)
- a hotel in a bakery
- a secret jazz concert in buildings designed by Gaudí
- the city's best churros
- the art of eating *calçots*, available only between January and March

Why do we love Barcelona?

- Because it's a city that feels like it's always on holiday: sun, beaches, outdoor drinks all year round.
- Because you'll find Banksy side-by-side with Gaudí; in this city, there's poetry everywhere.
- Because there are rooftops everywhere, and stairs and elevators on every street corner to take you there for a drink and to admire the city from above.
- Because the whole city is a party: from intimate neighbourhood gatherings (with human pyramids) to popular parties and clubs, Barcelona is the city of 'Fiesta Mayor'.

We tasted everything, searched high and low, and explored all over ... Here are our 30 favourite experiences to unlock Barcelona's secret doors, capture its heartbeat, and uncover its soul.

SYMBOLS USED IN **SOUL OF BARCELONA**

< 20 euros

20 to 60 euros

> 60 euros

you'll need a car
to get there

reservation
recommended

take advantage
of the terrace

staff, a bit rough around the edges, but that's part of the appeal

---

Opening times often vary,
so we recommend checking them directly
on the website of the place you plan to visit.

3
24
16
5
9
8
4
15
29
12
2
14
10
21
11
26
19
23
20
30
18
13
22
7
1
17
25
27
28

30 EXPERIENCES

01. A tiny establishment for tapas
02. The micro-city Casa Bonay
03. The art of eating *calçots*
04. Jazz to the rhythm of Gaudí
05. The *asador* that specialises in grilled meat and fish
06. Palo Market Fest, a market unlike any other
07. The tapas sanctuary
08. A pizzeria in a car park
09. Spend a night in a bakery
10. The best *patatas bravas* in Barcelona
11. Have a bath beneath the city
12. The Michelin-starred restaurant that's all about fun
13. The coolest private club in the world
14. The best bar in the world?
15. The temple of yoga
16. Barcelona's treasure trove
17. It's Vermouth o'clock
18. La Boquería market's pocket-sized restaurant
19. If you're a sucker for stationery ...
20. Where to grab a drink
21. The granny adored by top chefs
22. Hot chocolate and charcuterie
23. The best sandwiches in town
24. A modernist masterpiece, without the crowds
25. Enjoy a cocktail in a retro bar
26. The best massage ever?
27. To the end of the night
28. A relaxing stay in Poble-sec
29. Speciality coffees, vegan gastronomy and scandi-design
30. Behind the fridge, decadent cocktails

LOWENBRAU

#01

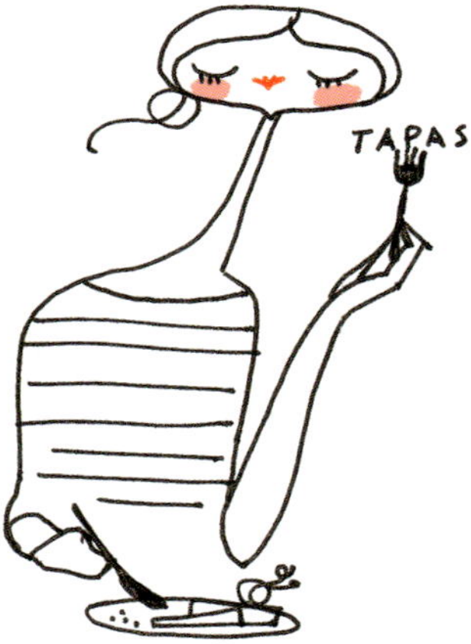

A TINY ESTABLISHMENT FOR TAPAS

Tiny, noisy, frenetic ... this pocket-sized bodega is an institution renowned throughout Spain.

You won't find any tables here – it's standing room only. Let yourself be tempted by a glass of the house vermouth as the tapas appear and disappear at full throttle. Red bell peppers, foie gras, camembert with honey, grilled artichoke, cod, sweet and savoury pintxo ... Quim's tapas are inspired creations – he nails it every time, and his daring recipes soon pop up all across the country. Some Barcelonians even call Quimet y Quimet the 'elBulli of tapas'.

Definitely don't skip the salmon with yogurt and honey truffles paired (de rigeur) with a glass of pink cava, a fresh and bubbly rosé that will banish all thoughts of prosecco from your mind.

QUIMET & QUIMET
CARRER DEL POETA CABANYES, 25

+34 934 42 31 42 | quimetiquimet.com

#02

THE MICRO-CITY
CASA BONAY

'Casa Bonay is more than just a hotel; it's a micro city' – as this opening line from an article in *The Telegraph* suggests, Casa Bonay is far more than a hotel: it's a coffee shop, bookshop (Barcelona's smallest), cocktail bar, several restaurants, rooftop bar... and, above all, a platform for all the local talent, since everything here is 100 % Made in Barcelona.

Ines Miró-Sans, the hotel's founder, trained at the Ace Hotel in New York so she knows better than anyone that a hotel is first and foremost a living space with a programme. Even if you aren't staying at the hotel, check out the events on its site: guest DJs at the weekend, documentary screenings, concerts, parties, curry nights, book presentations – you're bound to find what you're looking for to take a break at Casa Bonay.

CASA BONAY
GRAN VIA DE LES CORTS CATALANES, 700

€€

+34 935 458 070 | casabonay.com

ROSIE
REVERE
ENGINEER

Calçots
Estrella

Calçots

#03

THE ART OF EATING *CALÇOTS*

Each country has its culinary curiosities, and eating *calçots* will throw even periwinkle-eaters for a loop!

Calçot season – exclusively between January and March – is an unmissable gastronomic event for Barcelonians.

Calçots – elongated, sweet onions that look a bit like little leeks – are eaten grilled with Romesco sauce, a mixture of almonds, hazelnuts, tomatoes, and garlic. To die for.

It's when you get around to actually eating these famous *calçots* that things get interesting. There's a whole ritual involving donning a bib and setting aside any pretence of elegance and glamour.

SO HOW DOES IT ACTUALLY WORK?

Step 1 : Peel the skin off the grilled *calçots*. Obviously your hands are completely black now ... Barbecue style. Awesome.

Step 2: Dip the *calçot* in delicious Romesco sauce. This is the coolest part of the exercise.

Step 3: Dangle the full length of *calçot* over your head, open your mouth and aim for your piehole while trying to avoid making a total mess!

Step 4: Savour this delicate and finger-licking tidbit ... of slightly barbaric appeal.

You get the message: We love *calçots*. They're gourmet, addictive, fun to eat in company, and available only a few months a year – so, if you get a chance to try them, don't let it pass you by.

> EL MIRADOR DE CAN CASES
FOR FIRST-RATE *CALÇOTS*

Calçots are truly an insider's treat. Not many travelers even know they exist – not least because you can't get them everywhere. That's why we love this place on a hilltop just a few minutes drive from the city centre.

Not many tourists know about Mirador de Can Cases, so you'll find mostly locals, here to indulge in *calçots* and other grilled delicacies. Keep in mind that this type of onion is only available from January to March.

Miss this window and your belly might well be miffed – and you won't have anyone to blame for it but yourself.

EL MIRADOR DE CAN CASES
CAMÍ DE CAN CASES, 15
LES PLANES

+34 93 589 18 68

cancases.com/en

04

JAZZ TO THE RHYTHM **OF GAUDÍ**

The name Gaudí will never sound the same to you again after you've attended this magical jazz festival, which is held once a year in buildings designed by the nec plus ultra of Catalonian architects. A glass of champagne in your hand, jazz notes reverberating off modernist edifices beneath the stars ... What more could you ask for?

CASA BATLLÓ
LAS NOCHES MAGICAS
PASSEIG DE GRÀCIA, 43

€€

+34 932 160 306
info@casabatllo.cat

casabatllo.es/ca/venda-entrades/visita-nits-magiques

#05

THE *ASADOR* THAT SPECIALISES IN GRILLED MEAT AND FISH

Heads up: you're about to discover the city's best-kept culinary secret. Nothing beats starting your day with sweetbread toast and a good *café con leche*. Ultramarinos is one of those places that Spaniards call a *bar de toda la vida* – a typical bar that never changes, a little corner of paradise for local regulars.

Everyone cheerfully tosses their orders over the stainless-steel counter: *escabetx* of the day and marinated anchovies in the guise of tapas, chicken a la planxa as crispy as it's juicy, and above all meat grilled on the iconic *asador*. From *txuleta Ibérica* to *kokotxas al pil pil* and the gigantic fish of the day, it's impossible not to find your bliss here.

€€

ULTRAMARINOS MARÍN
C/ DE BALMES, 187, SARRIÀ-SANT GERVASI

+34 932 17 65 52 | ultramarinosmarin.com

CONCEPT
GALLERY

#06

PALO MARKET FEST, **A MARKET UNLIKE ANY OTHER**

Nothing would make you suspect that a market featuring Barcelona's most influential small creators is held once a month here, at the heart of this industrial neighbourhood.

From vendors of costume jewelry and more or less experimental fashion to up-and-coming DJs and obscure food – the melting-pot of creatives here today will give you a taste of the cultural and party scene of tomorrow.

These artists and artisans congregate here to see and be seen, so remember their names because you might stumble across the Cristóbal Balenciaga of the 21st century.

PALO MARKET FEST FLEA MARKET
CARRER DELS PELLAIRES, 30–38

palomarketfest.com

Instagram: palomarketfest

UNA PIZZ
UNA
PIZZA

PHOTO CREDIT: FANY PÉCHIODAT

#07

THE TAPAS **SANCTUARY**

Try to arrive early at Cañete so you can nab a spot at the narrow and neverending bar. It's the perfect spot for leisurely watching the cooks with their superb toques, who seem straight out of the animated film *Ratatouille*, and brisk waiters dressed in white whose enthusiasm is contagious. Guaranteed entertainment.

On the menu: *pan con tomate*, aubergine chips, *jamón de Bellota*, *gambas a la plancha*, artichoke omelette dusted with truffle ... Typically Barcelonian tapas, simple and potent recipes that put the emphasis on flavour and conviviality.

CAÑETE
CARRER DE LA UNIÓ, 17

+34 932 703 458 | barcanete.com

CAÑETE

PARKING PIZZA

#08

A PIZZERIA **IN A CAR PARK**

It may feel like you're entering a garage, but you'll definitely know you're in a pizzeria once you're inside: Welcome to Parking Pizza.

During the day, the loft-style industrial beauty of this space will surprise you with its calm and relaxing vibe. At night, you'll almost think you're in one of Berlin's underground clubs. The wood-oven cooked pizzas are delicious, especially the one with burrata and stracciatella.

And for a taste of the easternmost Mediterranean cuisine you can pop right next door to the pizzeria's 'little brother', Parking Pita.

€€

PARKING PIZZA
PASSEIG DE SANT JOAN, 56

parkingpizza.com | Instagram: parkingpizza

#09

SPEND A NIGHT **IN A BAKERY**

8 am. The light filters into your room. You open your eyes. You're barely conscious when the scent of croissants fresh from the oven lures you out of bed.

The alarm clock has just gone off at the Praktik Hotel in Barcelona. A hotel-cum-bakery that smells deliciously of oven-hot bread. The lobby? Right between the baguettes, pies, and cakes ... The elevator? At the back to the right, behind the chouquettes. The reception? At the end of the bread counter of the famous Baluard Barceloneta, the city's best bakery.

Less than 10€ will buy you a complete breakfast with all the bread and pastries you can eat. Good morning, Barcelona!

€€ / €€€

PRAKTIK BAKERY
CARRER DE PROVENÇA, 279

+34 934 880 061 | hotelpraktikbakery.com

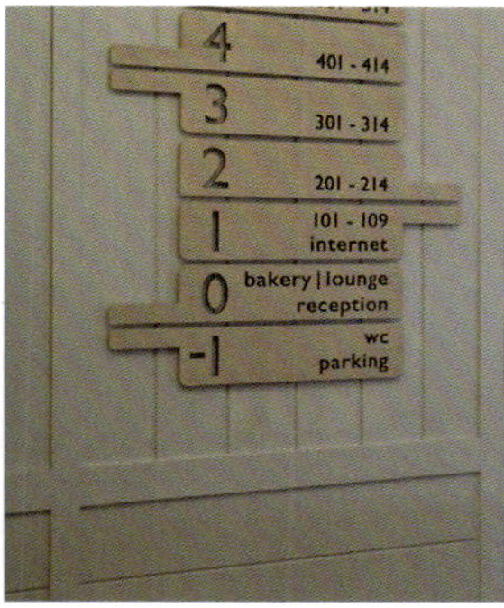
4 401 - 414
3 301 - 314
2 201 - 214
1 101 - 109
internet
0 bakery | lounge
reception
-1 wc
parking

clarel

#10

THE BEST
PATATAS BRAVAS IN BARCELONA

> EL TOMÁS

WHERE BARCELONIANS HAVE BEEN GOING FOR 40 YEARS

Located in the Sarrià neighbourhood, El Tomás is the kind of place that plays its cards close to its chest. Far from the trendy rooftops and bars, El Tomás de Sarrià is simply the place where, for 40 years now, all of Barcelona has been going for the city's best *patatas bravas*.

Hand peeled and cut, El Tomás's *patatas* are tender to perfection and served with a generous coating of aïoli or delicious chili sauce.

A little warning for nightbirds: El Tomás doesn't live on Spanish time and closes at 10 pm! So remember to come early so you don't end up having to go home hungry.

EL TOMÁS DE SARRIÀ
CARRER MAJOR DE SARRIÀ, 49

+34 932 03 10 77

eltomasdesarria.com

> LA MUNDANA
CONTEMPORARY *PATATAS BRAVAS*

Leave the Kinder eggs to the kids – presenting Tapas Surprise!

The menu at this confounding restaurant features dishes that are as traditional and integral to the Catalan identity as they come. But, while you may have ordered patatas bravas, it will take you a moment to recognise them when they appear in the form of an ultra-graphic chocolate or caramel eclair. Same thing for the paella, which shows up half-a-centimetre thick on a square surface but is still creamy and tasty.

Incredibly playful, this trompe-l'oeil cuisine is the fruit of the imagination of Alain Guiard and Marc Martín, who cut their teeth in Europe's most prestigious kitchens and have won numerous prizes for their catering service. Respected by all of Barcelona's great chefs, they've brought their talents and sense of humour together at La Mundana, where everything is faux traditional but genuinely exquisite.

€€€

LA MUNDANA
CARRER DEL VALLESPIR, 93

+34 934 088 023 | lamundana.cat

MUNDANA
DE SANTS
VERMUTERIA GASTRONÒMICA

TEPIDARIUM

#11

HAVE A BATH **BENEATH THE CITY**

While you're in Barcelona you might be tempted to indulge in some R&R. Luckily you can escape the noise of the city while staying right in the heart of it at this underground spa located in an 18th-century warehouse in the El Born neighbourhood.

In this sanctum dedicated to the pleasures of relaxation, several pools of various temperatures allow you to relax both body and mind, before or after a well-earned massage. What's more, this temple of wellbeing is open until 2am on Friday and Saturday and until midnight during the rest of the week. A getaway you should always keep in mind for after a long night of tapas.

€€

AIRE DE BARCELONA
PASSEIG DE PICASSO, 22

+34 932 955 743 | beaire.com

#12

THE MICHELIN-STARRED RESTAURANT **THAT'S ALL ABOUT FUN**

Inhalable whisky pie, edible cotton you can pick directly from the stalk, translucent pasta – this restaurant is all about having fun. This gourmet eatery rich in flavours and intensity is the brainchild of three former chefs from the acclaimed elBulli: Mateu Casaña, Oriol Castro, and Eduard Xatruch.

To ensure maximum enjoyment of their 30-dish cycle of gastronomic poems, the cooks won't let you look at the menu or google it in advance.

A disfrutar (= enjoy)!

€€€

DISFRUTAR
CARRER DE VILLARROEL, 163

disfrutarbarcelona.com

Tasting menu – 180 euros (without wine)

#13

THE COOLEST PRIVATE CLUB **IN THE WORLD**

Soho House is a members' club that's opening incredible spaces, reserved for creative and artistic talents, all over the world. Here, you can work, eat, sleep, and party with members, whose creativity seems to know no bounds.

Soho House has two locations in Barcelona:

- A hotel located in an 18th-century antique-pink building at the heart of the city's Barri Gotic (Gothic Quarter). Good news: the hotel and Cecconi restaurant are open to non-members (by reservation), so you can try their classic pasta alle vongole (with clams) and schmooze.

SOHO HOUSE
PLAÇA DEL DUC DE MEDINACELI, 4

+34 932 204 600

sohohousebarcelona.com

- The Little Beach House, located 30 minutes by car, near Garraf. Your mission: track down a member who'll invite you to eat paella as you dangle your feet in the water. Definitely worth a trip!

LITTLE BEACH HOUSE BARCELONA
CARRER MIRADOR DEL PORT, 1
GARRAF

+34 935 221 552

sohohousebarcelona.com

A BRIEF GUIDE
TO PAELLA

While the original recipe may be from Valencia, not all of its derivatives go by the name of paella: some are called *arroz* (rice) and others *fideuá* (because they're made with vermicelli).

To help you out, here's a brief guide to paella:

PAELLA: According to the traditional recipe, only vegetables (including artichokes, bell peppers, and tomatoes), green beans, *garrofó* (a type of large white bean), chicken, and rabbit go into this dish, which is originally from Valencia.

MEAT PAELLA: Generally contains primarily chicken, though you'll definitely also find other kinds of meat. This spicier version of the dish comes mainly from Spain's inland regions: a real country dish.

SEAFOOD PAELLA: Composed of squid, clams, mussels, prawns, and other seafood, it's sometimes even served with fish. Obviously, this version comes chiefly from the country's coastal regions.

IXED PAELLA: Combines meat and seafood, especially squid and prawns. This land-and-sea dish is also often found in France.

ARROZ AL HORNO: Unlike paella (which roughly means 'cooked in a pan'), this dish is cooked in the oven, with plenty of meat, sausage, and chickpeas.

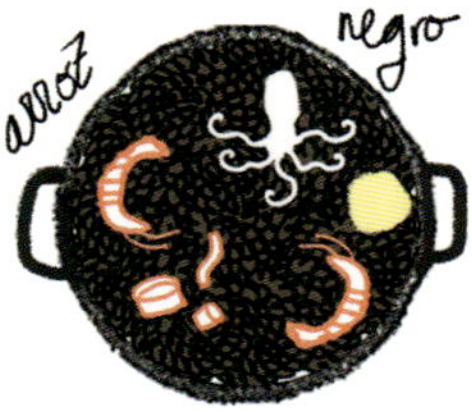

ARROZ NEGRO: This dish derives its characteristic colour from squid ink. A mix of squid, prawns, and garlic, it's usually served with aïoli.

FIDEUÁ: This may look like paella from a distance, but the squid, prawns, and mussels in this dish come with noodles and fish soup instead of rice. It's sometimes served with aïoli and never contains meat.

#14

THE BEST BAR IN THE WORLD?

While we don't always agree with the "50 best" rankings (far from it), we have to admit that they weren't far off the mark when Sips was voted The World's Best Bar in 2023 (after coming in 3rd in 2022).

We'll do you a little favour and not describe their most spectacular cocktails here. That way we won't ruin the surprise factor when the – inevitably delicious – cocktails arrive at your table. Just ask the waiters for their recommendations ...

The brainchild of Simone Caporale (World's Best Bartender in 2014) and Marc Álvarez (former bar manager for legendary restaurateurs Ferran and Albert Adrià), Sips opened in 2021.

Not to be missed.

€€

SIPS BAR
C/ DE MUNTANER, 108

sips.barcelona/drinkery-house | Instagram: sips.barcelona

#15

THE TEMPLE **OF YOGA**

Inhale, exhale ... and lick your lips. Frizzant is about more than just reaching 'relaxation nirvana' with vibrating oms in downward dog at the best yoga studio in town. It's also a culinary experience, with its own coffee shop serving morning stretchers with bulging mascarpone and matcha croissants, chai latte and delicious cold-pressed juices.

At lunchtime, local freelancers eat chicken with dates before perhaps indulging in the incredible *danzad malditos*, a very special ritual you can discover here every Tuesday at 6:30pm in the most delirious dance class you'll ever take.

€€

FRIZZANT
GRAN VIA DE LES CORTS CATALANES, 692

+34 93 17 04 96

frizzant.com

NIVEA
Orangen

#16

BARCELONA'S **TREASURE TROVE**

Just a stone's throw away from Barcelona lies the small town of Sant Cugat and its flea market. Here you'll find antiques dealers, artisans, and designers who will make you want to redecorate your entire apartment with the bargains you dig up here.

After wandering amidst a thousand and one decorative treasures you can sit down at one of the many tapas bars or food trucks – which are also inspiring and inspired in their design.

MERCANTIC
AV. DE RIUS I TAULET, 120
SANT CUGAT DEL VALLÈS

+34 93 674 49 50

mercantic.com

MERCANT

17

IT'S VERMOUTH O'CLOCK

Vermouth in Barcelona is like G&T in the UK: a classic pre-dinner drink, not to say an institution. So Barcelona's *vermuterías* are the equivalent of London's small pubs – but with a generous splash of Spanish sun!

Barcelona's best neighbourhood bar, Calders, has one of the loveliest terraces for enjoying a drink, served with olives, as is customary. You can sip it with a side of squid or other tinned tidbits.

If you head here after dark, we recommend arriving early so you can snag a nice table outdoors and order a special Vermouth menu – ensuring you'll make the most of the local happy hour.

CALDERS
CARRER DEL PARLAMENT, 25

+34 93 674 49 50

Instagram: barcalders

#18

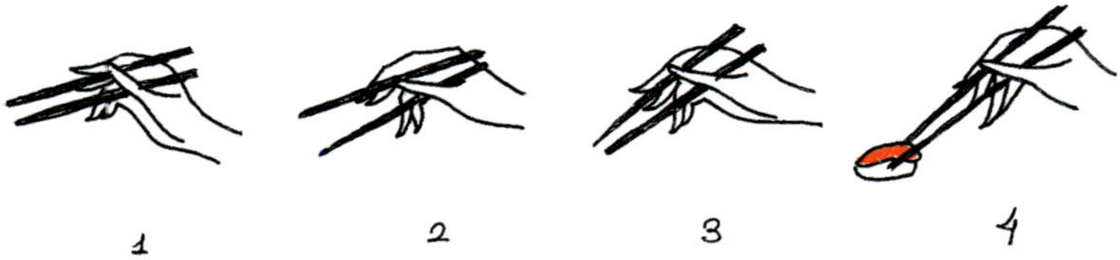

LA BOQUERÍA MARKET'S POCKET-SIZED RESTAURANT

Arnau Muñío, an erstwhile chef at the great elBulli, decided to open this restaurant of his dreams beneath the arcades of this Barcelonian market. He wanted to serve *cocina de mercat*: the sort of market cuisine his grandmother would cook using whatever she'd found at the stalls that day.

There are only eight seats around the small wooden counter to ensure that the unique menu gets its full due. Since sharing this sort of culinary adventure can only bring people closer together, there's a good chance you'll end up best friends with your neighbours at the table.

€€€

DIREKTE BOQUERÍA
CARRER DE LES CABRES, 13

direkte.cat

A QUICK TOUR
OF LA BOQUERÍA

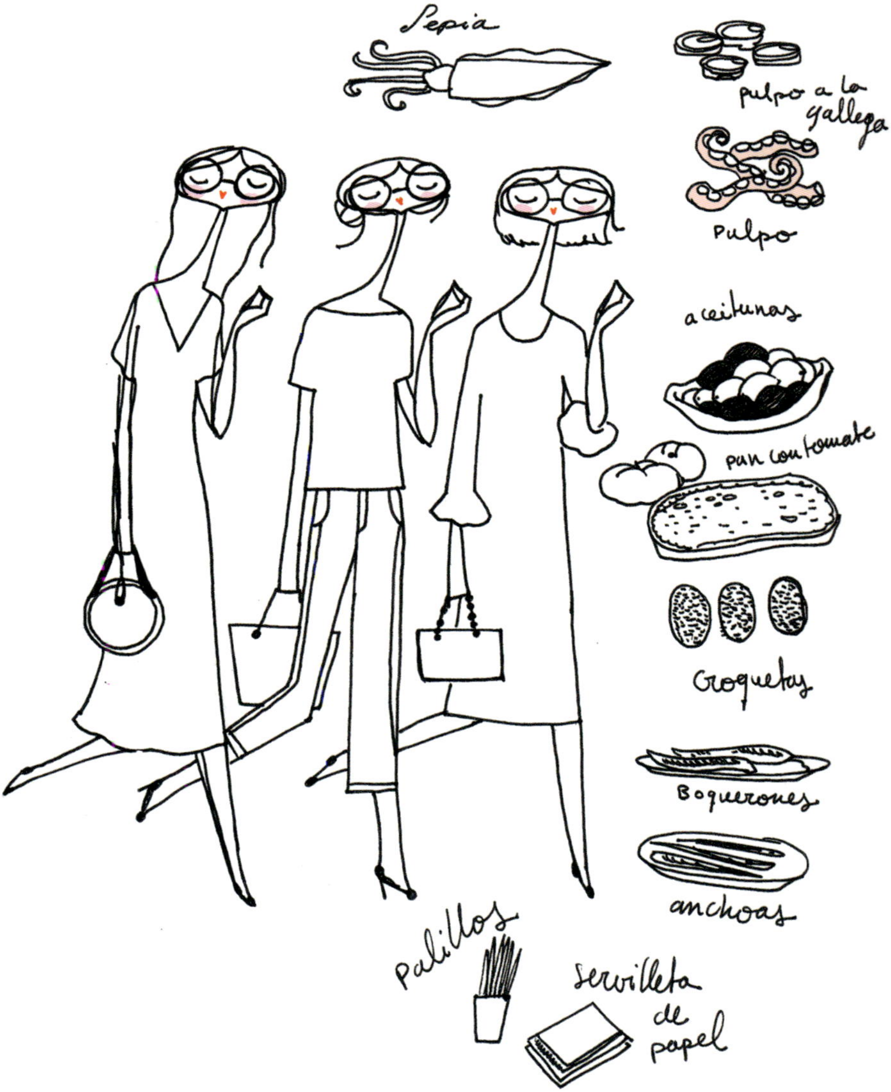

2,49
4,99
6,90

CAN VILA
La Jamonería

The temple of Barcelona, La Boquería is teeming with artisans selling fruits and vegetables, charcuterie, seafood, wine, and good preserved foods. You'll also find a tapas bar, street food that's beyond tempting, and food shops. Here are our top picks:

- Torrons Vicens. **405.**
  For stocking up on *turrón* (Spanish white nougat).
- Olives i conserves El Pinyol. **230.**
  For olives and quality preserved foods.
- Cansaladeria Can Vila. **162.**
  The *jamón* paradise.
- Embotits Montse. **173.**
  The nec plus ultra of Spanish delicatessens.
- Ous de Calaf. **323.**
  To help you decide between the chicken and the egg.
- Fruites i Verdures Vidal Pons. **512.**
  A greengrocer bursting with colours.
- Peixateria Manolo. **759.**
  A fishmonger specialised in oysters.
- Fantasía de Pimientos. **610.**
  The paradise of peppers, from sweet to spicy.

La Boquería has created this interactive map to help you find your way around, with more information about each stall: boqueria.barcelona/paradas-mercado

For a different kind of market with a less touristy atmosphere, head to La Concepció, the municipal market in Dreta de l'Eixample, which boasts a beautiful iron and wooden structure dating from 1887. Our favourite stops include Cut Fish, Fina y Coloma, Fruites Manolita and Tot Bo.

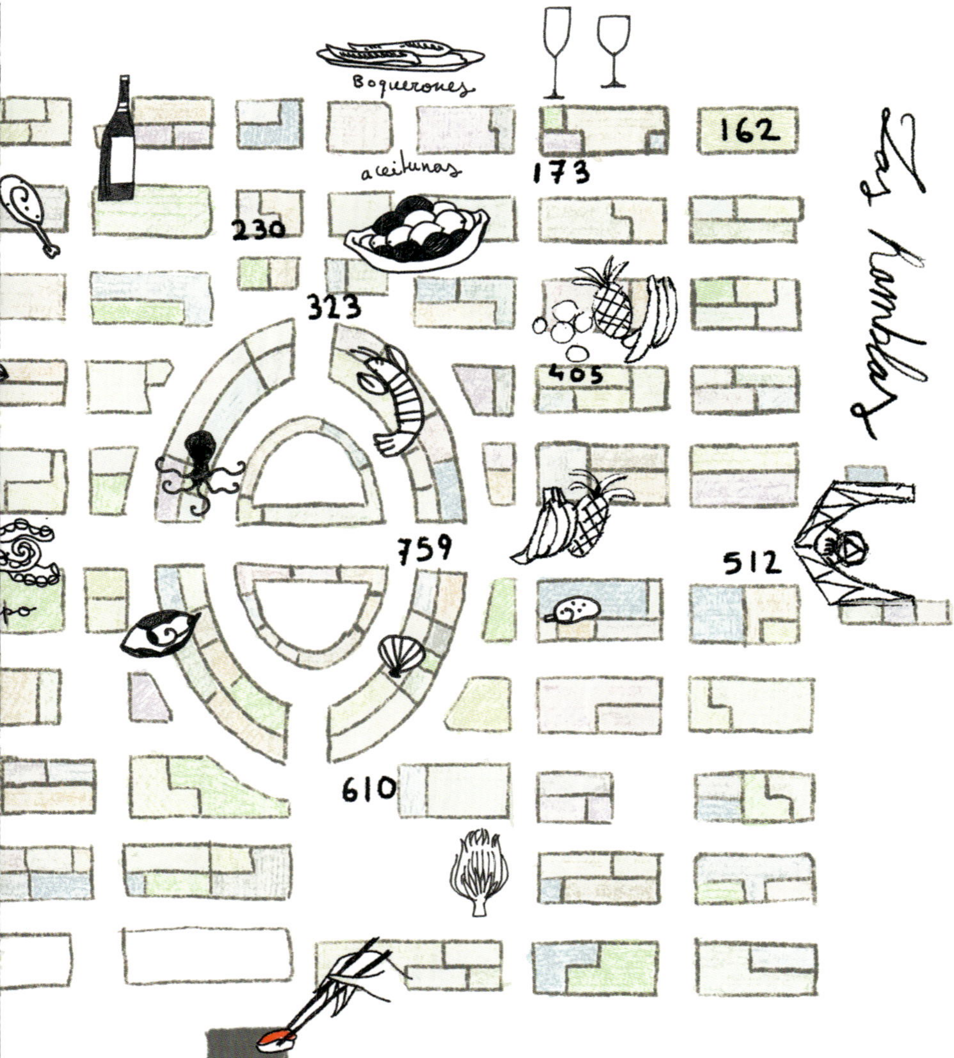
Boquerones
162
aceitunas
173
230
323
405
Las Ramblas
759
512
610

NO TOCAR
DON'T TOUCH
NO TOCAR
DON'T TOUCH

27
RAIMA
RAIMA
RAIMA

#19

IF YOU'RE A SUCKER **FOR STATIONERY ...**

Picture an ocean of notebooks, papers, pens, and pencils: Raima is, simply put, the biggest stationery shop in Europe. It was founded in 1986 by Núria Raja in this very building, which dates to 1913 – with many pieces of vintage and upcycled furniture that are still there to this day.

Don't forget to go up to the 4th floor, where you'll find a little-known terrace with a breathtaking view over the rooftops of this historic city.

RAIMA
CARRER COMTAL, 27

raimapapers.cat

#20

WHERE TO GRAB **A DRINK**

This wine bar-cum-dining cellar is embedded in the reactor core, on the thoroughfare that separates El Born and La Ribera. As soon as you enter, a long display table of wines gets straight to the heart of the matter. Next up is a second bar, followed by two rooms that share a third bar, which also serves as a 'serving hatch' for the open kitchen, where the chef keeps a watchful eye on every plate.

In short, you get the picture: This is the kind of chaotic place we love, rough around the edges but serving Barcelona's best natural wines. Bar Brutal also has the city's best *burrata* and other tapas that are as nummy as they are no-nonsense.

€€

BAR BRUTAL
CARRER DE LA PRINCESA, 14

+34 932 954 797

barbrutal.com

Bar Brutal
RACTIVO
ERITIVO
BORN
BE WI

va mejor
con
Coca-Cola
PEIX
PAN TOSTADO 180
CAL ROMANA 650
BOMBA 200
ARENGUE 250
MORCILLAS 390
SARDINAS 550
BARAT 600
BACON 200
CALAMAR
HABAS 240
PULPO 600
BUTIFARRA 360
RECORTES PULPO 400
CHORIZO 360
BACALAO 650
CAP i POTA
ESCABECHE 550
AMANIDA
JUDIAS
GARBANZOS
ENSALADILLA
TELLERINES

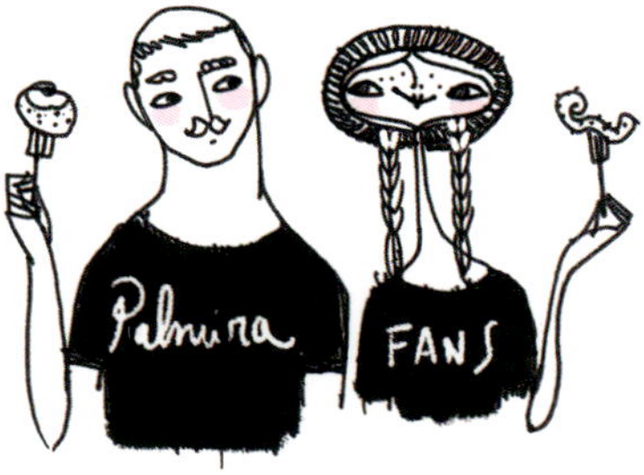

#21

THE GRANNY ADORED **BY TOP CHEFS**

This small family restaurant harbours a treasure that goes by the name of Palmira. In the guise of a rustic, irresistible little granny, she's actually one of the country's most respected chefs – that's how authentic she's managed to keep her cooking. Since she founded her establishment in 1944, all the top chefs have made pilgrimages there to (re)discover the taste of real traditional tapas, like their own grandmothers undoubtedly made.

Surrounded by her family, Palmira offers a short, no-frills menu that always features local and seasonal products – including bomba, breaded potato croquettes that'll knock your socks off. If they're in season, the artichokes will make your heart melt. The *alubias con sepia* (cuttlefish and beans) and *recortes de pulpo* (squid) are also well worth the trip.

LA COVA FUMADA
CARRER DEL BALUARD, 56

+34 932 21 40 61 | Instagram: la_cova_fumada

#22

HOT CHOCOLATE **AND CHARCUTERIE**

Don't let the modest façade and dated look fool you: Granja Viader is one of *the* main spots of Barcelona's culinary scene.

Founded in 1870, this erstwhile dairy is now an institution where Barcelonians cross paths with travelers who've come here to discover Granja's mythic hot chocolate, a thick and dense beverage topped with a generous dollop of whipped cream ....

GRANJA VIADER
CARRER D'EN XUCLÀ, 4

+34 933 183 486

granjaviader.cat

Granja M.Viader

Granja M.Viader
Cardedeu
SIMÓN COLL

You can pair this decadent indulgence with another sweet treat, from churros to *melindros* (ladyfingers), but definitely don't miss trying a slice of ham or piece of cheese with quince jam and a touch of fleur de sel. Absolute heaven.

Don't be surprised if you run into the Michelin-starred chef Albert Adrià since he's the one who told us about this somewhat secret spot, where he loves to have breakfast. For the record, Picasso himself came to Granja for hot chocolate ... The place where great connaisseurs converge.

P.CONESA
GALLETAS LOSTE
BOCADILLOS
CALIENTES
SURTIDO
FIAMBRES

#23

THE BEST SANDWICHES IN TOWN

Open since 1951, Can Conesa serves the best sandwiches in town, hands down.

Another plus is that it's just a stone's throw from the cathedral – an area that's otherwise short on quality eateries.

Choose from 70 types of sandwiches (don't hesitate to ask for recommendations from among the house specialities), have a seat in the small room next to the counter and tuck in.

€

CONESA ENTREPANS
CARRER DE LA LLIBRETERIA, 1
(PLAÇA DE SANT JAUME)

+34 93 310 13 94

conesaentrepans.com

#24

A MODERNIST MASTERPIECE, WITHOUT THE CROWDS

Love Art Nouveau but can't stand the tourists who swamp Gaudí's greatest hits and the Sagrada Familia? Then the exceptional former Hospital de Sant Pau, with its modernist architecture (as Art Nouveau is called in Spain), is for you.

Built between 1902 and 1930 by the architect Lluís Domènech i Montaner, the complex was home to the Hospital de la Santa Creu i Sant Pau from 1916 to 2009.

Far from the crowds in the historic centre, you can take unabashed delight in strolling through the gardens surrounding the various pavilions, some of which have been renovated and are open to visitors.

In particular, don't miss the former San Rafael Pavilion, the Hypostyle Hall and the magnificent mosaic around the building by Francesc Lavarta and Mario Maragliano.

An exceptional visit that's not to be missed.

RECINTE MODERNISTA DE SANT PAU
C/ DE ST. ANTONI MARIA CLARET, 167

The visit lasts between 1.5 and 2 hours

+34 93 511 78 76
santpaubarcelona.org

© THOMAS JONGLEZ

© THOMAS JONGLEZ

16
15

9
"EN ACCION DE GR
UNAS DEVOTAS D
VIRGEN DE LAS LAG

#25

ENJOY A COCKTAIL **IN A RETRO BAR**

Welcome to early 20th-century Barcelona, the perfect era for enjoying a cocktail made with flowers or peanuts. More than just a cocktail bar that uses exceptional ingredients, La Confitería 1912 is virtually a museum of Art nouveau- inspired decor.

You'll find another alternative for exploring Barcelona's raffish side a few blocks away at Bar Marsella.

LA CONFITERÍA 1912 CARRER DE SANT PAU, 128 (€€)	BAR MARSELLA CARRER DE SANT PAU, 65 (€€)
+34 931 40 54 35 confiteria.cat	Instagram: barmarsella

1888
1888
1888

THE
MASSAGE
HOUSE

#26

THE BEST MASSAGE EVER?

For some people, it's the best massage they've ever had. For others, it's an excellent treatment in an elegant and relaxing atmosphere.

Marc Oromí is an unparalleled therapist who combines various techniques: chiromassage, Thai massage, reflexology, Japanese facial massage and more.

What else is there to say? Just go – you won't regret it.

€€

THE MASSAGE HOUSE
PASSATGE MERCANTIL, 1, CIUTAT

+34 637 386 974

themassagehouse.es

THE MASSAGE HOUSE

#27

TO THE END **OF THE NIGHT**

1. DANCE TILL DAWN

Partying is fundamental to Barcelona. This city stays up long after the sun goes down, with the nightlife carrying on in bars and clubs it's hard to choose between. Here's our selection of places for carousing to the end of the night.

SALA APOLO
CARRER NOU DE LA RAMBLA, 113

2 rooms, 2 vibes
sala-apolo.com

JAMBOREE
PLAÇA REIAL, 17

Jazz club
jamboreejazz.com
MOOG

SIDECAR
PLAÇA REIAL, 7

300-person club
sidecar.es

CARRER DE L'ARC
DEL TEATRE, 3

Electro club
moogbarcelona.com

RAZZMATAZZ
CARRER DELS ALMOGÀVERS, 122

Barcelona's biggest nightclub, with 5 rooms
salarazzmatazz.com

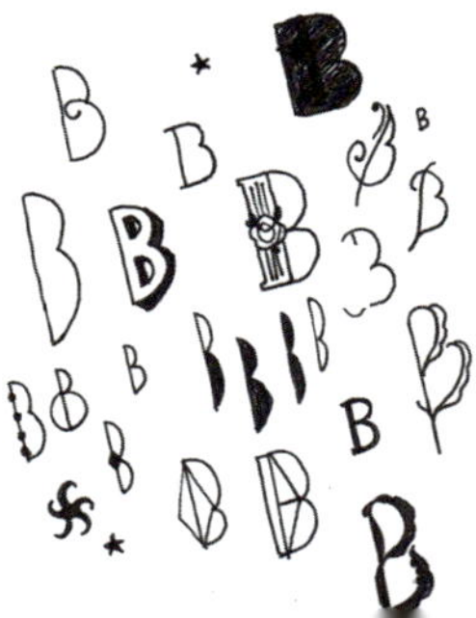

Fiesta

2. A CHURROS AFTERPARTY

> Churrería J. Argilés

This food truck right by the exit of the Marina subway station hasn't moved an inch in almost 60 years. Surrounded by streets and trams, Churrería J. Argilés's location itself is already an experience. Open 24 hours at the weekend, it's the perfect place to refuel after having danced the night away, especially since its churros are amongst the best in the city. Something the locals clearly know!

€

CHURRERÍA J. ARGILÉS
CARRER DE LA MARINA, 107

+34 932 32 43 07

> Churrería San Román

A Barcelona institution, this churrería is run by Manuel San Román, a family man who's been perfecting his personal recipe since he was 12-years old. In other words, his churros have been getting better and better every day for almost 50 years now – just to give you an idea of how perfectly crispy and tender each mouthful is. We recommend coming here early in the morning, as soon as the oil starts heating up – so you'll have the privilege of savouring the first batches of the day.

€

CHURRERÍA SAN ROMÁN
CARRER DEL CONSELL DE CENT, 211

+34 93 453 25 82 | churreriasanroman.com

3. ASPIRIN IN AN ART NOUVEAU SETTING

Yes, a pharmacy can be worth going out of your way for.

Farmacia Aguilar Pérez already stands out because of its modernist façade alone. Inside, in an interior covered with Art nouveau-style carved wood panels, you'll find everything you could need to help you recover from a paella overdose or long night out.

While we don't recommend it, we understand how incredibly tempting it is to take a few pictures. Ther again, they could have a placebo effect – that's how therapeutic the decor here is.

€

FARMÀCIA AGUILAR PÉREZ
CARRER D'AUSIÀS MARC, 31

+34 933 02 19 58

4. THE CITY'S CALENDAR OF EVENTS

Barcelona's neighbourhoods are a reflection of its *trencadís*: like mosaics, they each have their own personality, traditions, and above all festivals. With some luck, you'll have a chance to get to know the soul of these neighbourhoods and their inhabitants during your stay.

MARCH

> The weekend closest to 23 March: Barri del Pi.

APRIL

> Mid-April : Sagrada Familia.
> 23 April: Sant Jordi. World Book Day.

MAY

> 2nd half of the month: Eixample derecho.

JULY

> 1st half of the month: Vila Olímpica.
> 2nd half of the month: : Poblesec.
> Mid-July: El Raval.

AUGUST

> 2nd half of the month: Gràcia.
> 2nd half of the month: Sants.
> Mid-August: Barrio Gótico.

SEPTEMBER

> 1st half of the month: La Ribera
> 1st half of the month: Poblenou Primera.
> 1st half of the month: Horta.
> The week of 24 September: Fiestas de la Mercè. A major festival that happens across the entire city.

OCTOBER

> 1st half of the month: Sarrià.
> 1st half of the month: La Rambla.
> 1st half of the month: Eixample Izquierdo.

NOVEMBER

> 1st half of the month: El Clot.

THE ROOFTOPS OF BARCELONA

In Barcelona, it is of course impossible to go higher than the tallest tower of Sagrada Familia, which rises to 172 metres. Despite this limitation, Barcelona has many skyscrapers scattered throughout the city.

These include some with sublime rooftops from where you can admire Barcelona from on high.

1/ Located on a busy street, the Grand Central Hotel has a rooftop you can't detect from the outside. Dare to enter the hotel and proceed to the elevators to go up to the Skybar, where you can enjoy a glass of wine while you take in the view of the infinity pool and city.

2/ For a sky-high and festive evening, head to the rooftop of Hotel Pulitzer in summer (through late September). Five days a week, the hotel organises parties starting at 6 pm, with good music, tapas, and cocktails.

3/ The latest addition is the rooftop of the Barcelona Edition, where greenery and wooden elements make for a warm atmosphere.

1/ THE SKYBAR, AT THE GRAND CENTRAL HOTEL

2/ HOTEL PULITZER

3/ BARCELONA EDITION HOTEL'S ROOFTOP

28

A RELAXING STAY
IN POBLE-SEC

Tired of the crowds and touristy atmosphere in El Raval, El Born and Barrio Gótico? Then Hotel Brummell is the place for you.

With its perfect location at the foot of Montjuïc hill in the Poble-sec district (a mix of working-class neighbourhood and trendy spots), you'll feel right at home from the moment you arrive. The service is professional, young and friendly, the decor stylish, the rooms comfortable, and there's a small swimming pool to cool off in summer ...

El Raval is a 10- to 15-minute walk away (the metro is just five minutes on foot) and the area around the hotel is teeming with good bars and restaurants.

€€

HOTEL BRUMMELL
C/ NOU DE LA RAMBLA, 174
SANTS-MONTJUÏC

+34 931 25 86 22
hotelbrummell.brummellprojects.com

20 rooms

URBARNA
POSTCARDS

MENU VEGANO
DE LA SEMANA
LUNES
PEANUT NOODLES
MARTES
FOCACCIA
MIERCOLES
JUEVES
VIERNES
SANDWICH
DIRTY VEGAN
CLUB DE VINO NATURAL
HAZTE MIEMBRO HOY!

#29

SPECIALITY COFFEES, VEGAN GASTRONOMY **AND SCANDI-DESIGN**

Just a few blocks away from the hustle and bustle of downtown Barcelona, El Poblenou exudes calm even though the neighbourhood is booming. Here, abandoned warehouses have been given a new lease of life by creatives of all kinds: House of Rowdy for fashion, Garage Beer for beers brewed on site ...

This clutch of outstanding concept ventures includes Casa Taos, a hybrid coffee shop that promotes a taste for sustainable products. In this wood-clad urban shed, open to the street at all hours, you can enjoy speciality coffees, natural Catalan wines and vegan victuals, all served on Scandinavian-style designer furniture that's available to take away for the really keen.

€

CAFÉ CASA TAOS
C. D'ÀLABA, 100, SANT MARTÍ

+34 930 17 27 78

taosliving.com/blogs/casa-taos/prueba

BEHIND THE FRIDGE,
DECADENT COCKTAILS

On one side: a *pastrami* stand.

On the other: a secret cocktail bar. Just open the refrigerator door and take the secret passage to discover surprising flavours served in far-fetched glasses. You can definitely trust the mixologists when they recommend their craziest cocktail of the moment.

€€ / €€€

PARADISO
CARRER DE RERA PALAU, 4

paradiso.cat

Instagram: paradiso_barcelona

PARADISO

MANY THANKS TO

JÉRÔME for introducing me to Barcelona and for accompanying me on all my explorations.
NOÉ for unflaggingly tasting all the pasta in town.
VINCENT AND JUAN for enrapturing the soul of this city in drawing and image.
EMMANUELLE AND NATHALIE for doing and undoing this book with patience and passion.
XAVI ALBA for finding us tables that did not exist in Albert's restaurants.
THOMAS JONGLEZ our expedition leader.
And **ENRIC AYMERICH**.

This book was created by:
Vincent Moustache, co-author and illustrator
Fany Péchiodat, co-author
Berta de March, co-author
Carmen Vasquez, co-author
Juan Jerez, photographer
Nathalie Chebou-Moth and Roberto Sassi, publishing managers
Emmanuelle Willard Toulemonde, layout
Sophie Schlondorff, translator
Kimberly Bess, proofreading

You can write to us at contact@soul-of-cities.com
Follow us on Instagram on @soul_of_guides

In the same collection:

Soul of Amterdam
Soul of Athens
Soul of Berlin
Soul of Kyoto
Soul of Lisbon
Soul of Los Angeles
Soul of Marrakesh
Soul of New York
Soul of Rome
Soul of Tokyo
Soul of Venice

Cover: Photo Credit © Logan Armstrong – Unsplash

Registration of copyright: March 2024 - Edition: 02
ISBN: 978-2-36195-732-2
Printed in Slovakia by Polygraf